SONGS
ARE LIKE
TATTOOS

poems by

Elizabeth Majerus

Finishing Line Press
Georgetown, Kentucky

SONGS
ARE LIKE
TATTOOS

For Matt

ACKNOWLEDGMENTS

The poem "1971" appeared in the Spring 2012 issue of *Obsession Lit Mag.*

Publisher: Leah Huete de Maines
Editor: Christen Kincaid
Cover Art: Paige Spangler
Interior Art: Otis Mitchell
Author Photo: Veronica Mullins
Cover Design: Elizabeth Maines McCleavy

Order online: www.finishinglinepress.com
also available on amazon.com

Author inquiries and mail orders:
Finishing Line Press
PO Box 1626
Georgetown, Kentucky 40324
USA

Table of Contents

BLUE

A Case of You

I am a chaste little heretic,
and I keep my heart in a pretty thicket.
Thick set, we made it our home.

I traveled, thinking
to return,
but the branches grew dense
and brambled. I drew
a scattered map of Los Angeles, while you
studied the Thomas Guide.

Just before our love got lost
you said, "You are a rock. Who
wouldn't want to lay
their foundation on you?"

And I said, "If I am a rock, I guess
        you must be
        my church."
Then I tripped
            and fell.

Once we lived a hundred miles apart and spent
all weekend in bed. We read each other
naked poems in a twist of sheets.

When we lived in the same room,
we had to steal out to cafés
and become strangers to get into bed at all.

So long split, still glittering
chips of you litter me.

I seem immune,
still I carry you: A corner of the crease
in my smile, the brunt of my elbow,
the tart trim of my tongue.

Part of me can't stand the fact
that our tether is severed.
But I can't take a case
of you.   The best I can do is taste

a trace of you
          in these lines   from time to time.

River

Coming on   Cutting down
     Putting up
          Pieces of song

I had *I wish*   oh

Don't snow pretty   stays green
     Make crazy money, quit this scene

Oh   I had a river wish   So long

You tried   Put me
     Loved me so
Made me weak

I rivered my wish
     So long
I would   Teach my feet to fly

I'm hard   I'm selfish
     I'm so   Sad
Now I've gone   Now I've lost

The baby I never had

California

Say you go.
The place you swore with
a laugh you'd never live.
The land of lemony sunshine
where no one walks anywhere.
Except you.

How can you be sad here
where bougainvillea blooms
above gateways and bird of paradise brushes
your bare knees as you walk to work?

Say you love the flowers,
the avocados four for a dollar,
the painted ocean sunset sky.
Say you hate the beige box buildings,
the gushing and clotting of cars   cars   cars,
and the loneliness of a thousand acquaintances
passing for friends. No matter. You came here
for him—it will never be your home.
You came for love. And love isn't enough.

This man, boy. Who you jumped with bare
into the night lake, walked with down
every snaking path. Who filled your head
with music, let you teach him to sing.

And when it was time to fly off somewhere
together, it was Los Angeles.

You say, *Okay. For you.*
You say, *Next time, I pick the city.*

Bleach bright beauty,
warm days and cold nights.
You came for love. But this
love is not enough.

This Flight Tonight

Summers long   before you
Numberless days   unreal
          They stretched on
At fourteen   a little lifetime

To get to summer   I flew four hours
from O'Hare   to Spokane   Dad drop-off
          with a two-pound box of Fannie Mae
Mom pick-up   with blue chips and apple slices
          Milky tea and oat scones
                    at home   (other home)

In the air   in the middle,
I was wet-eyed, puffy-faced,
          practicing not giving a shit
what strangers think

The Police in my head
my walkman shrieking *O my God,*
you take the biscuit, pushing out
the chronic chatter of the plane

***

Summer after summer   with you,
          running away from you
We stayed   in school
Kept summer   unreal

Summer taught me to fly   so I fly
Bumped from coach   to first class   free champagne
(I never liked champagne)
Scruffy and paranoid   Nothing on me
but fear   some Guatemala City airport official
will know on sight   I'm lit
more than I ever meant to get

on an Apple-Pan-parking-lot LA layover
in your dark back seat

Royal Crescent Mob in my head, singing
Five more minutes with you
Our long moment   so over
those lines feel funereal

Thirty minutes outside the Apple Pan
is enough   for now

As you drove me back   to LAX
I was struck   six years   and we've never
taken off and landed together

***

Later   you're a past chapter
I'm in my last   unreal summer
Sick with choppy air and my first trimester
Everything gets real   real soon

I'm alone   not fully

Prince in my head   channeling Joni   singing
Help me, I think
I'm falling...
The call button rings   the light stays lit

This flight tonight   my last flight alone
Soon   to lap   or not to lap
sippy cups and board books
The no time   of air time
        (reading   writing)
becomes   working   to kill time
        (no reading   no writing)

to will it past and us all finally touching down on a coast

But I'll be missing   no one
Everyone dear   will be here
in my hair   and sucking up my air

The Last Time I Saw Richard

Last time I saw Richard he told me
he was the same man he'd ever been.
It was me who'd changed, he said,
gone all fragile and soft.

"You sit silent," he said, "That's not like you.
You used to lead the smart talk, now
you're just soaking it in. You'll get flabby
if you don't stay in the game."

He put three quarters on the back room table
at the Plaza Tavern, let me play the winner.
But he shoved my cue from behind as I set up
my shot. The stranger I was playing set
the skewed ball to right and I sank it.
The waitress squeezing by with her tray
asked, "You know that dick?"

"Richard, you *have* changed," I said,
"It's not just crust. Now there's a wall.
It's choking off your decency."
His eyes were all flint and no shimmer,
but I heard something catch
when he cleared his throat.

Richard was still married to the job, last I heard,
talking labor on his phone in line for coffee
by 6:30 AM. He drinks at home with his roommates
most nights, and they're all about the union, too.

Excuse me now while I rack these balls and crack
them clean and wide. I'm listening. I still soak
it in when there's a pocket of quiet. I'm an hour
late for home, but I'm alone and I've got to play
just one more game where I can hear the chalk squeak
and the bar talk, where every shot is mine.

All I Want

I'm on a lonely road. I love this lonely
you've loaned me, love. Sometimes I need me back
a moment. You know. You take the kids and *Go,
we're fine.* And I know. You kiss me go. I pack.

It's good. You wreck me in the best ways, right
me when I'm skewing. You piss me off, yes.
And then you listen. Hear my shrinky insights.
When things are fine you sing sublime nonsense.

Some days we go for weeks, passing notes
and passing off the youngsters—temperamental,
beautiful batons. Always, though, the flow
returns us, spooning, spinning words. Content.

Sometimes I trip on how happy we could be.
All we could be is what we are. You see?

My Old Man

Coffee in the can   sugar in the bowl
His arresting eyelashes   All the girls in fits, wands
waving   He is warm   against me
His slope familiar   His scent   swims me

I know   See there   a book in his hands
He sits and reads as the kids wheel about
Coffee cooling in the cup   sugar in the mouth
He lifts his eyes   his gaze   I grow   luminous

We are the solid fragments of his firmament.

He sits and tries to read as the kids wheel about
He grouses   I'm still charmed   or tolerant

He wakes in blue light
to soothe   nothing doing
I tread   like hovering
    an inch above the ground

He tells me all his troubles, all his troubles
Ten times he tells me all my charms

(We sometimes need to have
a bit of a chat.)

Little Green

She called you Leslie and kept
your birthday. She could not
keep you. Too young.

Younger still, I called you
seed that grows in darkness,
I called you *basement baby,*
called you *knock knock.*

I was too young to be told
the trouble. Strange months.
Why did our father hide her in the cellar
when company came?

She left, came back, talked to me
at last. When she told me your story,
your name, how you'd been stolen,
I knew. I already knew.

I was the only one invited
to her yearly rite. We crouched
near her closet, laid hands on a brand new
birthday dress, just bigger than last year's.

She held you a long moment
against her bound breasts, then
the nun unwound you from her arms.
She came home empty handed.

All my young life I imagined
someday a miraculous return.
Now I know there won't be one.

As you keep your own orbit
somewhere, what bits of her
do you body forth?

She is lost to us. You answer
to some other name.

Carey

The winds up from the Sahara
have made a mess of my tidy room
and a nest of my hair.
I walk through dusty streets
in the sandals you made me,
sandals you'd make for anyone
with a ready twenty in hand.

This is not my home.
I have wandered here, a sand grain
escaped from a clutching hand,
and found you with your strong brown back
turned always in my direction.

Don't you know me? You must
have heard my name. You cook and dance
and measure a drunkard's feet
in this café that pulses with song
while I stand along the wall,
waiting for an in.

I step forward, sweeping up shards
of white plates dashed
in mad abandon.
You smile, accept the dustpan,
                smash the broken pieces back to the floor.

Your cave, its ancient bones, stolen eggs
scrambled on a camp stove. You are feral, but not
without reflection.

I'm struck by the way you tip
your silly cane.
There's a demon in your eyes, nomad.
I want that bite.

I need to be grabbed like a good old guitar and played hard,
not stroked like a fine thing lifted from a velvet box.

Some murder in this midnight air
won't let me sleep.
I will come to you, uninvited.

Blue

Dear you,
who know me
so far from me.
Dear you who
no longer know me at all.

There are opening notes
of songs that make
my body believe
I will see you soon,
in maybe five days. Notes rising
take me back to the ache
of five more minutes
with you.

The years   the years
        we are not   in touch.

You jostle my mind nearly
every day. When I say
        you   are in   my bones,
it's not pretty.

But this song is not about you.

Me, I am
in love   with the world,
wretched hell,   brilliant home.

Right now, I have someone
under my skin. A voice only,
a voice that didn't want to be
anyone's ghost.

But now that voice is mine
more than you are, my ghost,
and less.

What makes us go?
desire   *desire*   *desire*
                  the longing

                            for the dance

I turn from this voice, this new
ghost. I put on *Blue*.
Notes rising and falling
seep into me,
underneath the skin
and deeper.

Songs are like tattoos.
And you, fading,
a strong black line
turned a blurry blue.

MIXTAPE

what would Joni Do?

Put the Needle in the Groove

1.

Slow, low: those opening notes.
The kick drum hits you
In the thick of the heart.

Do you still feel this?

Plucked, ringing—strummed,
Filling the hall of your chest.
The spaces between chords
Rush you—bliss, ache,
glimmering heartbreak.
The voice ragged
At the seams, rips
shimmering in the melody.

Watch out: There's sugar everywhere.
Blood and salt tears.

2.

What I want I've got—
The fit of my palm
in the trank of its snug glove.

He wrecks my stockings,
kisses me weak after seven
thousand kisses.

But—
      but.

This settled heart tends fire.
The smolder of a song
buried. Burning peat
beneath the fields.

Can you hear the ghost, the groan
of those low notes? Wait
for the part where the toms roll
strong and spare and slow—
the sound of heart scar
not quite healed over.
Over and over.

Flip the record over.
Lift the tone arm from its cradle.
From beginning to end
to beginning, again.
Let the turntable spin.

A Portrait

When she was two feet off the ground she collected broken glass and bats. When she was three feet off the ground she made drawings of animals and forest fires. When she was four feet off the ground she began to dance to rock 'n' roll and sing the top 10 and bawdy service songs around camp fires and someone turned her on to Lambert Hendricks and Ross, Miles Davis, and later Bob Dylan. Through the vertical ran brief spurts of the church choir, Grade One piano, bowling, art college, the twist, a marriage, runs in the nylons and always romance—extremes in temperature and mirages.

Velvet Moon

I will get drunk alone tonight
on wine that's not delicious.
It has an alluring label,
an iridescent red moon.

I drink in your honor, my old
drunk friend. I am never alone
anymore. My time is his and hers
and all of theirs. Tonight alone

I get drunk on red wine and blue
ink, royal fountain. Splatter.
I'm making a small scene, my fingerprints
all over everything. I miss you.

I cry in my cups because I want to
be drunk with you, so far away.
I cry: if you were here, we would drink tea.

I'm out of your league. You'd leave
me behind, creep off with some
worthier drunk, some smeary one,
funnier and not so cooked as me.

I feel your grip on my elbow,
steering me back to myself. I'm uncorked
enough to call you, but not enough
to leave a message.

Bearded Heart

Unlucky one, lord
of my sandy passions,
you rejoiced to find yourself
encircled by my arms of abalone,
tied to my bearded heart.

We spent the summer braided
in your backyard hammock,
and winter found us tucked in,
sipping soup from one mug.
But spring brings mischief. I followed
the wind. I got stirred.

I was the slippery fish
trussed into bride clothes,
the one true true one
sent to you by some blundering god
who couldn't count.

You wept in your whiskey.
You plunged yourself
in work, wholesome work.
You are a town of your own
again, walled in by difficult wisdom.
You did not lose. You did not win.

I forgot you, you think. But it is not you
who are thinking about the tree, how
it was struck by lightning. It's me.

1971

I was a cellophane wrapper
on a pack of cigarettes.

I hid nothing, I couldn't
pretend to be strong.

Who knew I knew that raw
could turn me strong

that going deep would get me
free that I could make me.

My self—my songs.
One strong thing.

Extremes in temperature
and mirages.

I smoke as I breathe.
It clears my head and takes me

deep. I've picked up
a rasp. My voice smokes.

It would be easy to say I've become
the cigarette. But no.

It's in my hands, it serves
me. Smoke is my lover.

It scorched a hole in my throat.
It may kill me, it may not.

I will never
give it up.

Mixtape

Crack open the case. Slide out the tape. Find
traces of my brain, bits slivered from the pith
of my heart. I pass them to you. These tracks
send me into the milk of the moon, beyond
the pink, straight down the honey-dripped
bottleneck of sorrow, sad and soothing, up through
a heavenful of glimmery thrill that gets me up
off my ass, on the good foot. Each risky gift
irreplaceable, endlessly redubbable, stitched
together for you. I hope they'll send you too.

You made me mixtapes. Remember? You made me
twenty-two. You know you have a permanent piece
of my medium-sized American heart. You staked
your claim with "Five More Minutes." I came back
with "The Long Cut," a promise I was bound
to break. Someone asked, "Why don't you come
on back from way out west?" but that wasn't you.
Someone said, "What makes your big head
so hard?" and that sass, that sly regard,
is deep now in my inner grooves.

There is no you. You're snips of songs, silvered things
that ring in me. And I know there's no me, for you.
Still, you have a permanent piece, real estate.

The mixtapes keep coming. Yes: keep sending me,
you and you and you. Each with a track
or two that rends me, sends me seeking
who next to let get under my skin.

Songs are like tattoos.

And I'll keep sending mine
to you. And you, and you.

Whoever you may be, receiver, she
is on every mix. Kissing a Sunset pig,
knitting you a sweater. She's a free man
in Paris. Or she's sitting, waiting
for her sugar to show. Listening
to the silence and the radio. She's in there, big
and brave, breakable and verging on wavering
away, but always back, landing on rock.

Songs are like tattoos. Me and you fade
into each other's blue, move forward, mending.
Ready to be broken anew.

LINER NOTES

A Case of You
>"Just before our love got lost you said,"
>"I drew a map of Canada," and
>"taste a trace of you in these lines from time to time"
>>—Joni Mitchell, "A Case of You," *Blue* (Reprise, 1971)

River
>Fragments of "River," *Blue* (Reprise, 1971)

This Flight Tonight
>"O my God, you take the biscuit"
>>—The Police, "O My God," *Synchronicity* (A&M, 1983)
>"Five more minutes with you"
>>—Royal Crescent Mob, "Five More Minutes with You," *Spin the World* (Sire, 1989)
>"It was Joni singing 'Help me, I think I'm falling'"
>>—Prince (quoting Joni Mitchell, "Help Me") in "The Ballad of Dorothy Parker," *Sign O the Times* (Warner Brothers, 1987)

The Last Time I Saw Richard
>"Last time I saw Richard"
>>—Joni Mitchell, "The Last Time I Saw Richard," *Blue* (Reprise, 1971)

All I Want
>"I am on a lonely road"
>>—Joni Mitchell, "All I Want," *Blue* (Reprise, 1971)
>"Sometimes I trip on how happy we could be"
>>—Prince, "If I Was Your Girlfriend," *Sign O the Times* (Warner Brothers, 1987)

My Old Man
>"He tells me all his troubles and he tells me all my charms"
>>—"My Old Man," *Blue* (Reprise, 1971)

Carey
> Some details come from the Matala, Crete, sections of the biography *Will You Take Me As I Am: Joni Mitchell's Blue Period* by Michelle Mercer (Free Press, 2009)

Blue
> "The years… the years"
>> —Jane Siberry, "Dancing Class," *No Borders Here* (Duke Street Records, 1984)
>
> "didn't want to be anyone's ghost"
>> —The National, "Anyone's Ghost," *High Violet* (4AD, 2010)
>
> "desire, desire, desire / the longing for the dance"
>> —Stanley Kunitz, "Touch Me," *Passing Through: The Later Poems, New and Selected* (W. W. Norton, 1995)
>
> "five more minutes / with you"
>> —Royal Crescent Mob, "Five More Minutes With You," *Spin the World* (Sire, 1989)
>
> "underneath the skin… songs are like tattoos"
>> —Joni Mitchell, "Blue," *Blue* (Reprise, 1971)

Put the Needle in the Groove
> "He wrecks my stockings"
>> —Joni Mitchell, "All I Want," *Blue* (Reprise, 1971)
>
> "This heart's on fire"
>> —Wolf Parade, "This Heart's On Fire," *Apologies to the Queen Mary* (Sub Pop, 2005)

A Portrait
> Found poem drawn from an interview with Joni Mitchell by Marci McDonald ("Joni Mitchell Emerges from her Retreat," *Toronto Star*, February 9, 1974)

Velvet Moon

"my old drunk friend"

—Freakwater, "My Old Drunk Friend," *Feels Like the Third Time* (Thrill Jockey, 1994)

Bearded Heart

"But it is not you / who are thinking about the tree, how / it was struck by lightning. It's me."

—After "The Printed Page" by Jack Anderson, whose single stanza reads, "I am not now thinking about the tree struck by lightning. / It is you / Who are thinking about the tree, how / It was struck by lightning." (*Vital Signs: Contemporary American Poetry from the University Presses*. Ed. Ronald Wallace: University of Wisconsin Press, 1989)

1971

"I felt like a cellophane wrapper on a pack of cigarettes…I couldn't pretend in my life to be strong"

—Joni Mitchell describing the *Blue* period in an interview with Cameron Crowe ("Joni Mitchell," *Rolling Stone*, July 26, 1979)

Mixtape

"the milk of the moon"

—Mina Loy, "Songs to Joannes" [1917], *The Lost Lunar Baedeker* (The Noonday Press, 1996)

"on the good foot"

—James Brown, "Get on the Good Foot" (Polydor, 1972)

"You know you have a permanent piece of my medium-sized American heart."

—The National, "Looking for Astronauts," *Alligator* (Beggars Banquet, 2005)

"Five More Minutes with You" [song title]
  —Royal Crescent Mob, from *Spin the World* (Sire, 1989)
"The Long Cut" [song title]
  —Uncle Tupelo, from *Anodyne* (Sire, 1993)
"Why don't you come on back from way out west?"
  —Big Star, "Way Out West," *Radio City* (Ardent Records, 1974)
"What makes your big head so hard?"
  —Louis Jordan, "Caldonia" (Decca Records, 1945)
"Songs are like tattoos"
  —Joni Mitchell, "Blue," *Blue* (Reprise, 1971)
"kiss a Sunset pig"
  —Joni Mitchell, "California," *Blue* (Reprise, 1971)
"knit you a sweater"
  —Joni Mitchell, "All I Want," *Blue* (Reprise, 1971)
"a free man in Paris"
  —Joni Mitchell, "Free Man in Paris,"*Court and Spark* (Asylum, 1973)
"sitting…waiting for my sugar to show. Listening to the silence and the radio."
  —Joni Mitchell, "Car on a Hill," *Court and Spark* (Asylum, 1973)

Elizabeth Majerus is a poet, musician, and teacher, and she lives in Urbana, Illinois, with her family. Her poems have appeared in journals including *Another Chicago Magazine, The Madison Review,* and *Rhino Poetry.* She is one third of the band Motes.

www.ingramcontent.com/pod-product-compliance
Lightning Source LLC
LaVergne TN
LVHW041327080426
835513LV00008B/622